FASCINATING FACTS from the BIBLE

by Jeff Rovin

Introduction

Although there are many well-loved and familiar stories in the Bible, there are many historical pieces of information that are not as well-known. Drawing from both the Old and New Testaments, this book is filled with fascinating facts you'll want to share with everyone you know.

For example, the first man was called Adam because in the Hebrew language, the word means "man" or "mankind." When God brought Adam to life, he was bringing all humans to life.

And did you know that it wasn't Moses who told the Pharaoh to "Let my people go"? It was actually Moses' brother Aaron who did the speaking for Moses.

Here's another interesting fact: The common phrase "The Lord giveth and the Lord taketh away" is not found anywhere in the Bible. What the Bible actually says, in Job 1:21, is "Naked came I out of my mother's womb, and naked shall I return thither: The Lord gave, and the Lord hath taken away."

Why is the Bible called
"The Bible"?

Our word Bible comes from the Greek word *Byblos,* which was the name of the city in Phoenicia that produced papyrus – the early form of paper – for the Greeks.

The word *biblia* was then coined to describe little books, and since the Scriptures are essentially that – a collection of little books – the word Bible was used to describe them.

Who was the first
Christian martyr?

In Acts 6:8, a good man named Stephen became "full of faith and power" and went about preaching the word of Jesus. But certain powerful persons began to fear that he was trying to "change the customs" by which they lived. Thus, they "stirred up the people" against him. By Acts 7:58, the people were so irate that they "cast him out of the city, and stoned him."

Stephen's body was claimed by "devout men" and was buried with honor.

What commonly used word
originated in the Bible?

"Armageddon," meaning an apocalyptic battle, is perhaps the most famous word that comes from the Bible. It's origin is Har Megiddon, "the mountain of Megiddon," where many battles were fought in the Old Testament (Judges 5:19).

It's presumed that the final conflict, between the hosts of Heaven and Hell, will likewise be fought there...a battle that will be called Armageddon (Revelation 16:16).

What was John the Baptist almost named?

Before the birth of his son, Zacharias was visited by the angel Gabriel and told to name his son John. Unfortunately, the angel's appearance so startled Zacharias that he lost his voice.

When his wife Elisabeth gave birth, friends gathered around and suggested that she name him Zacharias, after his father. Elisabeth suggested John, but the neighbors argued that was hardly a traditional family name. She was on the verge of naming the babe Zacharias when her husband demanded a tablet and wrote, "His name is John."

His will was done, and Zacharias miraculously recovered his voice (Luke 1:5-25, 57-64).

How many bodies of water did God part?

There was the Red Sea, of course, which God parted with "a strong east wind" (Exodus 14:21). But He also caused the River Jordan to part – not once, but twice.

The first occasion was when the Children of Israel crossed the waters into the Promised Land of Canaan (Joshua 4:23). God caused the river to dry up so "that all the people of the Earth might know the hand of the Lord, that it is mighty." A stone altar stood for many years to mark the site of the crossing.

The second time was when the prophets Elijah and Elisha needed to get to the other side (2 Kings 2:8). Elijah struck the waters with his mantle, causing them to divide "hither and thither."

Who was the first person to get drunk in the Bible?

That honor belongs to Noah.

After the Ark settled on dry land, Noah and his sons Shem, Ham and Japheth emerged with their families. According to Genesis 9:20-23, one of the first things Noah did was "he planted a vineyard: And he drank of the wine, and was drunken." In his zeal he also doffed his clothing, though Shem and Japheth thoughtfully covered him as he lay in his tent.

Are there any books of the Bible in which God is not mentioned?

Incredibly, there are two books of the Bible in which the Lord is not mentioned at all: the Song of Solomon and the Book of Esther.

The former is understandable, as it's a comparatively short poem about love and beauty. However, not mentioning God in the latter is curious, since it is an extensive tale of the bold 5th century B.C. Jewish queen, the wife of King Ahasuerus of Persia, and her conflicts with the evil Haman. Or perhaps the Good Book is trying to tell us something: The only individual in the Bible who defeats wickedness unaided is a woman!

In contrast, one of the shortest books of the Bible, the one page Book of Obadiah, mentions God seven times.

How many commandments are there?

There are, of course, the famous Ten Commandments which God wrote upon "two tables of stone." But there are actually a total of 613 commandments in the Law of Moses, most of them collected in Leviticus. Included among these is the famous, "Thou shalt love thy neighbor as thyself" (Leviticus 19:18).

Delilah did not administer the most famous haircut in history

She did cause it to happen, however.

The mighty Danite hero Samson was the burden of the Philistines – so much so that five Philistine leaders promised Delilah 1,100 pieces of silver if she would learn the secret of his strength. Samson and Delilah became lovers, whereupon Samson was "vexed unto death" by her questions until he finally revealed, "If I be shaven, then my strength will go from me."

However, after Samson fell asleep in Delilah's lap, she did not cut his hair. Rather, "she called for a man, and she caused him to shave off the seven locks of his head" (Judges 16:19).

A peek into the future

The Bible doesn't make very many specific predictions about the future, though Daniel 11:3-4 hit one squarely on the head.

The verses state: "And a mighty king shall stand up, that shall rule with great dominion, and do according to his will.

"And when he shall stand up, his kingdom shall be broken, and shall be divided toward the four winds of heaven; and not to his posterity, nor according to his dominion which he ruled."

These and subsequent verses accurately describe the short reign of Alexander the Great, who was the king of Macedonia from 336 B.C. to his death 13 years later, at the age of 32. When he died, his empire was divided more or less equally among four of his generals.

A word to the wise.

And what do the wise do? They –

❦ "Gathereth in summer." – *Proverbs 10:5*

❦ "Holdeth his peace." – *Proverbs 11:12*

❦ "Harkeneth unto counsel." – *Proverbs 12:15*

❦ "Heareth his father's instruction."
   – *Proverbs 13:1*

❦ "Depart from the snares of death."
   – *Proverbs 13:14*

❦ "Disperse knowledge." – *Proverbs 15:7*

❦ "Shall have part of the inheritance among the brethren." – *Proverbs 17:2*

❦ "Loveth his own soul." – *Proverbs 19:8*

❦ "(are stronger) than ten mighty men which are in the city." – *Ecclesiastes 6:19*

Were the Philistines really such philistines?

Hardly.

The Philistines were relatively cultured and, more importantly, they had mastered the science of working with iron. This gave them an edge in manufacturing, as well as in warfare. They were the chief enemies of Israel from roughly 1200-1000 B.C., when David ended their stranglehold of the region.

It is from the Philistines that the region takes its present name: Palestine.

Psalms 14 and 53 – deja vu or a mistake?

Biblical scholars do not know why Psalms 14 and 53 are virtually identical. Some think it goes back to the time when Bibles were copied by hand, and an ancient scribe simply wrote it twice. Others believe it wasn't an error, but rather was intended as a "refrain" to be read aloud by a congregation.

Speaking of the Psalms...

Or rather, singing of them: Many of the subheadings such as "A Song of Loves" (Psalm 45), "Remembrance" (Psalm 70), and "Sabbath Day" (Psalm 92), apparently refer to specific melodies which, unfortunately, are lost to us today. (Note: Many Bibles combine Psalms 9 and 10, which means the numbering in your Bible may be off by one.)

The lost books of the Bible...

The Bible refers to a number of books which, alas, no longer exist: "Is not this written in the book of Jasher?" (Joshua 10:13) and "It is written in the book of Jasher" (2 Samuel 1:18); "it is said in the book of the Wars of the Lord" (Numbers 21:14); "written in the book of Shemaiah the Prophet" (2 Chronicles 12:15), and others.

Some scholars believe that these books never really were parts of the Bible, but were non-authorized writings by contemporary figures.

The writing was on the wall

A rather obscure event in the Bible gave us one of our most popular phrases.

In Daniel 5:1-31, the 6th century B.C. King Belshazzar of Babylon threw a great feast, attended by his family and a thousand nobles. During the festivities, "fingers of a man's hand" appeared and wrote a warning on the wall. No one could understand the words, and the Hebrew mystic Daniel was brought in to translate them. Daniel explained that the words – *Mene, Mene, Tekel, Upharsin* – spelt doom for the king. Sure enough, the writing was on the wall: That night, Belshazzar was assassinated and Darius the Mede became king.

Just what was Daniel doing?

What awful treason did Daniel commit that got him thrown into a lion's den?

He prayed.

An official in the court of Babylon, Daniel attracted the anger and envy of those who served King Darius. Knowing that Daniel prayed to God three times a day, the Babylonians persuaded their king to declare that for 30 days everyone was to worship only Darius. Naturally, Daniel disobeyed and was placed in the lions' den; its entrance sealed with a stone.

To everyone's surprise, Daniel emerged uneaten the next morning, explaining, "My God hath sent his angel, and hath shut the lions' mouths" (Daniel 6:22).

Who married a prostitute and why?

In the 8th century B.C., God wished Hosea to wed the prostitute Gomer so that, through her infidelities, he would feel God's pain. The Lord was upset at the way the Israelites had betrayed Him, how they "played the harlot" by worshiping idols and sinning.

Thanks in large part to his painful personal life, Hosea became a very vocal prophet of disaster, warning how the Israelites "have sown the wind, and they shall reap the whirlwind" (Hosea 8:7).

Seek and ye shan't find!

Nowhere in the New Testament does it mention the names or the number of the Wise Men who followed the Star of Bethlehem. Indeed, only Matthew refers to them at all, saying that "there came wise men" (2:1). We infer there were three men because they brought gifts of "gold, and frankincense and myrrh" (2:11).

Tradition (helped along by movies like *Ben Hur*)

has it that the names of the Wise Men were Melchior, Gaspar and Balthasar.

Born again

Jesus' resurrection is the most memorable and surely the most significant in the Bible, though it is not the only return from the dead – not by a long shot.

In the Old Testament, the prophet Elijah raised a widow's son from the dead (1 Kings 17:21-22), while the prophet Elisha brought back the son of a grieving couple (2 Kings 4:35); a dead man placed in the grave of Elisha also returned to life when his body touched the prophet's bones (2 Kings 13:21).

In the New Testament, Jesus raised both the daughter of Jarius (Luke 8:54-55) and Lazarus (John 11:43-44), while Peter revived Tabitha (Acts 9:40-41), and Paul did the same with Eutychus (Acts 20:9-12). The death and rebirth of Eutychus were particularly humiliating, since he'd been listening to Paul preach, fell asleep beside a window, and died when he "fell down from the third loft."

The shortest verse

The shortest verse in the Bible is John 11:35, which consists of two words: "Jesus wept."

How did he ever remember their birthdays?

The most-married man in the Bible was King Solomon, who had 1,000 wives: Seven hundred

were concubines who caught his eye at one time or another, while 300 of them were princesses, many of them given by their fathers to strengthen political or military ties.

The woman with the most husbands (although not all at the same time) was a nameless wife in Matthew 22:25-26. She married seven brothers, each of whom died in turn.

Fishers of men

The fish was used as both a secret code and an anti-Roman symbol by those who were persecuted in the early days of Christianity.

Why a fish? Not, as one might expect, because in Matthew 4:19, Jesus said, "Follow me, and I will make you fishers of men." Rather, it was because each of the letters in the Greek word for fish, *ichthus,* are the same as the initials in the phrase *Iesous Christos Theou Huios Soter*: Jesus Christ, of God the Son, Savior.

Don't stop the presses!

Cambridge University Press has been printing Bibles continuously since 1591 – longer than any other publisher in the world.

The first printed Bible, of course, came from Johann Gutenberg's newly invented printing press in 1456.

Very Old Testament

The oldest known fragment of Biblical text dates from 587 B.C.

The short passage is the Blessing of Aaron

(Numbers 6:24-26), and it's engraved on a pair of silver medallions discovered in Jerusalem in 1979:

The Lord bless thee, and keep thee:

The Lord make His face shine upon thee, and be gracious unto thee:

The Lord lift up His countenance upon thee, and give thee peace.

What was used to make the manger?

Most likely, the manger in which Jesus was born wasn't made of wood: Wood was extremely scarce in the area and was certainly not plentiful enough to make a structure of this type.

St. Jerome, among others, believes that the manger was constructed of mud or clay, as were many sheds and troughs of that time and place. Moreover, excavations in the region have unearthed similar structures made of those substances.

Exactly how tall was Goliath?

According to 1 Samuel 17:4, the Philistine of Gath stood "six cubits and a span" in height, which makes him just over nine feet tall.

When he faced little David, he was clad in a brass helmet, a massive coat of metal plates and brass leggings, and carried a spear with a heavy iron head.

Though it's well-known that David felled the giant "with a sling and with a stone," the blow appears only to have stunned Goliath. For in 17:51, it says that after the giant fell, David ran

over, took the Philistine's own sword, "drew it out of the sheath thereof, and slew him, and cut off his head therewith."

The Numbers Game – 7 and 666

For various reasons, the number seven is considered holy and perfect, beginning with Genesis 2:2: "And on the seventh day God ended His work." In other words, the perfection of creation had been achieved. Later, in Genesis 4:15, God says that "whosoever slayeth Cain, vengeance shall be taken on him sevenfold." Meaning that God's vengeance will be utter and complete.

Other sevens include the number of each clean beast and fowl Noah was instructed to take on the Ark (Genesis 7:2-3), the number of ewes in a special pact between Abraham and Abimelech, the length of time the Hebrews were to eat unleavened bread (Exodus 12:19), the number of deadly sins, the number of Angels of Revelation (with their seven vials of the seven last plagues), and more.

Scholars believe that "six hundred threescore and six" is said to represent the ultimate evil (Revelation 13:18) because however many times sixes are placed in succession, they will never equal seven – and, thus, the number will always be imperfect and corrupt.

Why did three days pass before Jesus rose from his tomb?

In Matthew 12:40, Jesus told the Pharisees and Sadducees, "For as Jonah was three days and three nights in the whale's belly; so shall the Son of man be three days and three nights in the heart of the earth."

The length of time was significant. Jonah was swallowed for trying to flee God's order that he preach in Nineveh, the capital of the Assyrian empire. His reappearance and reformation meant that he would go to Nineveh and inform the city that it would repent its sins or be destroyed.

Jesus rising from the dead after three days was intended to symbolize much the same thing for all of humankind.

Interestingly, it doesn't appear to have been three full days that passed between Jesus' death and resurrection. It was a custom, at the time, to count as a full day any portion of the day: Jesus died late in the afternoon on Friday and was gone from his tomb early Sunday.

What's new?

Nothing under the sun, according to the Bible.

In the short book Ecclesiastes, the Preacher notes early on that "there is no new thing under the sun" (1:9), and uses the expression another 24 times to show how tiresome life can be.

The phrase "the sun also ariseth" also comes from this book (1:5). It was lightly modified by author Ernest Hemingway to serve as the title for one of his best-known novels, *The Sun Also Rises*.

Chariots of fire

Hemingway wasn't the only one to turn to the Bible for a title. The motion picture *Chari-*

ots of Fire took its name from the phrase in 2 Kings 2:11 describing Elisha's ascent to Heaven – though it was not the chariot of fire but a whirlwind which bore the prophet upward.

Fiery chariots also appear in Isaiah 66:15.

It's a dog's world!

Though dogs are mentioned two dozen times in the Bible, cats aren't referred to at all. The only place you'll find a cat mentioned – and then, just once – is in the Apocrypha, in the Letter of Jeremiah.

Even relatively obscure animals like partridges, boar and gazelles are mentioned more often than cats!

Jewel of the Bible

There may be a scarcity of cats in the Bible, but there are many mentions of "cat's eyes" – along with dozens of other gems and precious stones. Among the many mentioned are amethysts, pearls, emeralds, diamonds, topaz, sapphires, rubies, sardonyx, beryl and more.

What is manna of bread?

Manna, the "bread from Heaven" sent by God to the Israelites in the wilderness, wasn't actually bread.

It appeared in the morning "when the dew that lay was gone up" (Exodus 16:14), and it is said to be "like coriander seed, white; and the taste of it was like wafers made with honey" (16:31). Whether it came from God directly or indirectly (as a type of fast-growing moss or produced, like honey, by insects) isn't known. However, the Israelites clearly hadn't seen anything like it before, since the words *man huh* mean "what is it?"

The Bible's faults

There are also more earthquakes than cats: The Bible mentions over a dozen by name, beginning with 1 Kings 19:11 and concluding with the killer in Revelation 16:18, described as "a great earthquake, such as was not since men were upon the earth, so mighty an earthquake, and so great."

The naked truth

Among the many odd deeds performed by prophets, one of the strangest was Isaiah's habit of walking through Jerusalem utterly naked — not just for an afternoon or even for several days, but for three years. According to Isaiah 20:3-4, the prophet did so as "a sign" that the king of Assyria would conquer Egypt and Ethiopia and lead away "captives, young and old, naked and barefoot, even with their buttocks uncovered."

Blood money

Judas was paid 30 pieces of silver for betraying Jesus, though he threw the money to the ground before running off to hang himself.

The priests who gave him the money did not know what to do: Deuteronomy 23:18 forbids ill-gotten gain from being brought "into the house of the Lord thy God," yet there the money lay.

They decided to take the pieces of silver and, after discussing it, "bought with them the potter's field, to bury strangers in" (Matthew 27:7).

When did Christians first become Christians?

For years, followers of Jesus still considered themselves to be Jews. According to Acts 11:26, it wasn't until years later, in Antioch (in what is now Turkey), that "the disciples were called Christians."

Who is buried in David's tomb?

Well, it isn't David.

The Tomb of David on Mount Zion in the hills of Jerusalem, is approximately a thousand years old, built some 1,800 years after the death of the great king. In fact, no one knows where David's remains lie.

The confusion stems from the fact that Mount Zion is where David built his first city. Any structure standing there thus "belongs" to the king.

Where was the Tower of Babel?

The tower where "the Lord did there confound the language of all the earth" was located in Babylon. Babel is simply the Hebrew name for the ancient capital of Babylonia in southwest Asia.

Our modern word "babble," which means a confusion of sounds or words, comes from the old English word "babele" which came from Babel.

Incidentally, archaeologists believe that the ruins known as the Entemanamki Ziggurat (a terraced, pyramid-shaped tower) is in fact, the famous Biblical tower.

What does my dream mean?

Imprisoned with the Pharaoh's butler and baker, Joseph interprets their dreams for them. In Genesis 40:13, he tells the butler, "Within three days shall Pharaoh lift up thine head, and restore thee unto thy place."

Moments later, in 40:19, he informs the poor baker, with heartless irony, "Within three days shall Pharaoh lift up thy head from off thee, and shall hang thee on a tree." Joseph adds rather cruelly that, just as the baker fed the Pharaoh, so shall he feed the birds – with his dead body!

Words to live by

Other famous sayings from the Bible include the following which, despite their familiarity, are well worth remembering:

- "How are the mighty fallen!"
  – 2 Samuel 1:19

- "Ye are the salt of the earth."
  – Matthew 5:13

- "The race is not to the swift."
  – Ecclesiastes 9:11

❦ "Thy word is a lamp unto my feet and a light unto my path."
– *Psalms 119:105*

❦ "He that is without sin among you, let him first cast a stone at her."
– *John 8:7*

❦ "For everything there is a season, and a time for every matter under heaven."
– *Ecclesiastes 3:1*

❦ "Judge not, that ye be not judged."
– *Matthew 7:1*

❦ "Greater love hath no man than this, that a man lay down his life for his friends."
– *John 15:13*

❦ "Blessed are the peacemakers, for they shall be called the children of God."
– *Matthew 5:9*

❦ "A divided household falleth."
– *Luke 11:17*

❦ "The spirit indeed is willing, but the flesh is weak."
– *Matthew 26:41*

❦ "The truth shall make you free."
– *John 8:32*

❦ "Man doth not live by bread alone."
– *Deuteronomy 8:3*

❦ "Render therefore to Caesar the things which are Caesar's, and to

God the things which are God's."
– *Matthew 22:21*

❧ "Whatever a man soweth, that shall
he also reap."
– *Galatians 6:7-8*

❧ "Can the Ethiopian change his skin
or the leopard his spots?"
– *Jeremiah 13:23*

❧ "A prophet is not without honor, but
in his own country."
– *Mark 6:4*

What else was in
the Ark of the Covenant?

According to legend, in addition to the tablets
of the Ten Commandments, the Ark of the
Covenant also contained a bowl filled with manna
as well as Aaron's rod. The Ark resided in
Solomon's Temple until it was razed by the Babylonians in 586 B.C.

The Ark's whereabouts thereafter are not
known.

What is the first commandment
found in the Bible?

It's this, from Genesis 1:28:

"Be fruitful and multiply, and replenish the
earth, and subdue it: And have dominion over
the fish of the sea, and over the fowl of the air,
and over every living thing that moveth upon
the earth."

Going straight

The New Testament provides us with the name of just one street: The Lord tells Ananias to "go into the street which is called Straight" in Damascus (Acts 9:11) to find a man named Judas. (Not *that* Judas: This Judas had had Paul as a houseguest.)

Straight Street can still be found today in Damascus.

Just where is Noah's Ark?

Many people believe that the remains of Noah's Ark will be found on the 17,000-foot tall Mt. Ararat. However, this belief is based on a misreading of the Bible.

In fact, what the text of Genesis 8:4 tells us is that the Ark came to rest "upon the mountains of Ararat," meaning that it could be on any of the many peaks in the vast Turkish range.

He had a dream

Dreams are frequent and important occurrences in the Bible. Often, they are God's way of speaking to his servants.

The very first dreamer was Abimelech, who, in Genesis 20:3-8, was informed that he must give Sarah back to her husband Abraham. The King of Gerar had accidentally taken her as his own, mistakenly believing that she was Abraham's sister.

27

Idol talk

Traveling through the desert after leaving Egypt, the Hebrews created a "molten calf" to worship (Exodus 32:4). For this sin, they were made to wander for 40 years before reaching the Land of Milk and Honey.

But the Bible tells us that these Israelites weren't the only ones who fashioned golden idols.

Perhaps the most outstanding idol maker was Jeroboam. After the death of Solomon, the king's domain was divided into the kingdoms of Judah and Israel, which were ruled, respectively, by Rehoboam and Jeroboam. Jeroboam was an old enemy of Solomon, an overseer who had plotted to wrest power from the King.

In 1 Kings 13:1-4, we're told that once he became king, Jeroboam erected idols and small sanctuaries to make religion more accessible to his subjects and also to keep them from going to Solomon's Temple in Judah. When God caused Jeroboam's arm to become paralyzed, he repented.

Maachah, mother of Judah's King Asa, made an idol (1 Kings 15:13), King Ahaz of Judah made several (2 Chronicles 28:2) and, for that matter, in both Numbers 21:9 and 2 Kings 18:4, we're told that Moses himself "made a serpent of brass" (albeit at God's request, to cure the sick) and that "the children of Israel did burn incense to it." Many years after the death of Moses, an irate King Hezekiah shattered the brazen snake.

Who was the apple of God's eye?

It was Jacob. In Deuteronomy 32:10, we learn that God "found him in a desert land, and...He led him about, He instructed him, He kept him as the apple of His eye."

Though this was the origin of that popular phrase, the use of the word "apple" appears to have been a long ago mistranslation of the word for "core." To be kept in the core – or center – of God's eye accurately describes Jacob's place of honor.

Holy masses!

According to Exodus, it was an incredibly large number of ex-slaves that Moses led from Egypt: "about six hundred thousand on foot that were men, beside children" (12:37).

Contrary to what is pictured in art and in motion pictures like *The Ten Commandments*, the children of Israel left Egypt at night (12:33, 42). Many scholars suspect that this was not just because Pharaoh sent them "out of the land in haste" in an effort to stop the 10th plague, the plague of death. They believe that Moses wanted to leave by moonlight because it would be necessary to pass the Egyptian fortresses of Migdol and Baalzephon, and he didn't want angry soldiers firing arrows and throwing spears at his people.

Star light, star bright

Despite its undeniable importance to the story of the birth of Jesus, the Star of Bethlehem is mentioned just once in the Gospels. In Matthew 2:2, the Wise Men say, "Where is he that is born King of the Jews? For we have seen his star in the east, and are come to worship him."

Let's get it right

Another famous saying from the Bible has been somewhat altered over the years.

In Proverbs 13:24, we are told, "He that spareth his rod hateth his son: But he that loveth him chasteneth him betimes."

No one knows how or when the saying became "Spare the rod and spoil the child."

What goeth before a fall?

Perhaps the oddest change of phrase from the Bible is "Pride goeth before a fall." What the Bible really says, in Proverbs 16:18, is "Pride goeth before destruction, and a haughty spirit before a fall."

What is really the root of all evil?

It isn't money.

What the Bible really says, in 1 Timothy 6:10, is "The love of money is the root of all evils."

A practical man

In 2 Samuel 12:13-23, David learns that because he committed adultery with Bathsheba, his son must die.

The king is despondent and, when the boy falls ill, the king refuses to eat or rise from the ground. After seven days the infant dies and the king's servants fear to tell him, lest he do something rash.

Much to their surprise, however, David is up and about, cleaned and ready to eat.

Explaining the change, David says, "While the child was yet alive, I fasted and wept: For I said, Who can tell whether God will be gracious to me, that the child may live?"

"But now he is dead, wherefore should I fast? Can I bring him back again?"

After the boy's death, Bathsheba bears David a new son: Solomon.

Picture this...

The Bible is full of graphic descriptions of God's wrath, such as "ye shall eat flesh...until it come out at your nostrils" (Numbers 11:18-20).

However, the authors also displayed a talent for vivid imagery, as in Isaiah 22:18 where it says rather more playfully that God "will surely violently turn and toss thee like a ball into a large country."

Here are more common Bible phrases...

🐛 "Out of the mouth of babes." – *Psalms 8:2*

🐛 "There is no new thing under the sun." – *Ecclesiastes 1:9*

🐛 "And they shall beat their swords into plowshares." – *Isaiah 2:4*

🐛 "Seek, and ye shall find." – *Matthew 7:7*

🐛 "The signs of the times." – *Matthew 16:3*

🐛 "Many will be called, but few chosen." – *Matthew 20:16*

Murder, they wrote

The Bible tells of many deaths – as well as the deaths of many.

The most destructive event was a battle between the Israelites and the Syrians, which resulted in 100,000 Syrian deaths (1 Kings 20:29-30). Retreating, the unlucky foe tried to enter the city of Aphek, only to have a wall collapse and kill 27,000 more men!

Not all of the great deaths occurred as a result of warfare, however, as recounted in 2 Samuel 24:12-15. Angered when David takes an illegal census, God offers him three choices: "Shall seven years of famine come unto thee in thy land? or wilt thou flee three months before thine enemies, while they pursue thee? or that there be three days' pestilence in thy land?"

David chose the pestilence, clearly underestimating the damage it could do as it claimed 70,000 men.

The runners-up for the most-deadly events include David slaying another 62,000 Syrians (2 Samuel 8-10), God killing 50,070 citizens of Beth-shemesh for daring to look upon the Ark (1 Samuel 6:19), and the Gileadites slaying 42,000 Ephraimites as they tried to leave the country. The Gileadites identified Ephraimites by ordering them to utter the word shibboleth, which they pronounced differently from the natives (Judges 12:5-6).

Despite the fact that God commanded us to take an eye for an eye and no more, the most excessive act of revenge in the Bible was displayed by the Israelites. Following the murder of a concubine by the Gibeans, the Israelites retaliated by slaying 25,000 Benjamites, who had given the killers safe haven (Judges 20).

I guess I'll be going

After Adam and Eve had sinned and were driven from paradise, God made sure they wouldn't return by placing "at the east of the garden of Eden Cherubims, and a flaming sword which turned every way" (Genesis 3:24).

God also made it clear that nothing or no one except Moses was ever to set foot on Mt. Sinai. In Exodus 19:12-13, He says, "Whosoever toucheth the mount shall be surely put to death; there shall not an hand touch it, but he shall surely be stoned, or shot through; whether it be beast or man, it shall not live."

Reader digests

God occasionally requests a show of faith from His people, whether it's Abraham sacrificing his son or Moses returning to Egypt to free his people.

But surely one of the strangest requests in the Bible was one God made of Ezekiel: In Ezekiel 2:8-10, God commands that the prophet "open thy mouth, and eat that I give thee." To Ezekiel's surprise, he was given a book.

After regarding the situation for a moment, Ezekiel says in 3:2, "So I opened my mouth, and He caused me to eat that roll." It tasted "as honey" and, more importantly, it gave the prophet all the words that God wished him to speak in the house of Israel.

But they're high in protein

While the Bible forbids us from eating a number of foods, there is one animal we are permitted to eat — presumably, if we're really hungry.

In Leviticus 11:22, we are told, "Even these of them ye may eat; the locust after his kind, and the bald locust after his kind, and the beetle after his kind, and the grasshopper after his kind."

Yum.

Can I have a bite?

Incredible as it may seem, though "a great company" came to be with Jesus at the Sea of Galilee, only one person, a youngster, had had the foresight to bring a snack.

According to John 6:1-11, seeing the hungry "multitude," Jesus took the boy's five barley loaves and two small fishes and after "he had given thanks," he distributed the food — which turned out to be more than enough for everyone.

Hunky dowry

The greatest wedding present in the Bible was the city of Gezer, given to Solomon when he married the daughter of the Pharaoh (1 Kings 9:16).

That was the good news. The bad news was that the Egyptian ruler hadn't wanted the city and had burned it to the ground and slaughtered all of its residents. Still, Solomon accepted the gift graciously and rebuilt the city.

What was it that destroyed Sodom and Gomorrah?

Many people mistakenly believe that God sent an earthquake to bring down the sinful cities, but this is not true. Genesis 19:24 is very explicit in stating that the destruction came from above: "The Lord rained upon Sodom and upon Gomorrah brimstone and fire from the Lord out of heaven."

Jesus' first miracle

The first of the 14 healing miracles Jesus performed was in Capernaum, when he cured the nobleman's feverish son (John 4:47-53).

What medicines did He use?

Jesus used no medicines of any kind — other than his own saliva!

In Mark 7:32-35, Jesus went to Galilee where he was introduced to a man who was deaf and suffered from "an impediment in his speech." Jesus first "put his fingers into his ears, and he spit, and touched his tongue," and the man was cured of both afflictions.

Later, in Mark 8:22-24, Jesus visited Bethsaida and a blind man was brought to him. And when Jesus "had spit on his eyes, and put his hands upon him," the man was able to see.

Passing another man who had been blind from birth, Jesus stopped and, in John 9:6, "spat on the ground, and made clay of the spittle, and he anointed the eyes of the blind man with the clay." After washing in the pool of Siloam, the man was able to see.

The strangest funeral
in the Bible

King David battled with Saul, but his hatred did not extend to Saul's son, the military leader Ish-bosheth. When Ish-bosheth was decapitated in his bed by officers who thought they were doing David a favor, the king was so furious that he ordered the killers' hands and feet lopped off and the men hanged.

As for Ish-bosheth, according to 2 Samuel 4:12, the king "took the head of Ish-bosheth, and buried it in the sepulchre of Abner in Hebron."

This is the only instance in the Bible of a head being buried without the body. Presumably, the body was buried where the men had left it.

Pigs that taste good...

As if bug eating weren't off-putting enough, Isaiah 66:17 recounts a rather odd meal stolen by one hiding behind a tree in a garden: Not only did the individual consume the forbidden "swine's flesh," but also a mouse.

...and pigs
with good taste

Both Matthew (8:31-32) and Luke (8:27-33) tell the story of Jesus' encounter with a man possessed by devils. Fearing that they would be driven out, the devils spoke to Jesus and asked that they be allowed to leave their host and take up residence in a herd of pigs that were feeding nearby.

Jesus agreed, but no sooner had the devils moved to their new home than the pigs "ran violently down a steep place into the lake, and were choked."

Who had the longest name in the Bible?

According to Isaiah 8:1, that unique honor belongs to the son of the prophet: Maher-shalal-hash-baz.

What is the most common name in the Bible?

There are over 30 Zachariahs, with Azariah a runner-up at nearly 30. Third place goes to Meshullam, of which there are over 20.

An Abram by any other name...

Many people in the Bible change their names after they have been transformed by some important event. This was true from the time of Jacob, who became Israel (Genesis 32:28), to the days of Simon and Saul, who were renamed Peter and Paul when they became apostles of Jesus.

However, the most significant name change was when Abram made his covenant with God in Genesis 17:5, 15.

To show his devotion, Abram added part of the sound "Yah" (Hebrew for "the Lord") to his name and became Abraham.

His wife Sarai did likewise and became Sarah.

Capital punishment

The Bible is very clear about the crimes that are punishable by death.

Execution awaited any who:

🌾 "Smiteth (strike) a man, so that he die."
   – Exodus 21:12

🌾 "Smiteth his father, or his mother."
   – Exodus 21:15

🌾 "Stealeth a man, and selleth him."
   – Exodus 21:16

🌾 "Curseth his father, or his mother."
   – Exodus 21:17

🌾 "(Be) a witch." *– Exodus 22:18*

🌾 "Lieth with a beast." *– Exodus 22:19*

🌾 "Sacrificeth unto any god, save unto the Lord only." *– Exodus 22:20*

🌾 "Doeth any work in the Sabbath day."
   – Exodus 31:15

🌾 "Giveth any of his seed unto Molech."
   – Leviticus 20:2

🌾 "Commiteth adultery with another man's wife." *– Leviticus 20:10*

🌾 "Lieth with his father's wife."
   – Leviticus 20:11

🌾 "Lie with his daughter-in-law."
   – Leviticus 20:12

🌿 "Lie with mankind, as he lieth with a woman." – *Leviticus 20:13*

🌿 "Hath wrought folly in Israel, to play the whore in her father's house." (applied to any daughter who is not a virgin and weds) – *Deuteronomy 22:20-21*

🌿 "Take a wife and her mother." – *Leviticus 20:14*

🌿 "Profaneth herself by playing the whore." (applied to the daughter of any priest) – *Leviticus 21:9*

🌿 "Hath spoken to turn you away from the Lord your God." – *Deuteronomy 13:5*

🌿 "Is stubborn and rebellious (and) is a glutton and a drunkard." (applied to a son) – *Deuteronomy 21:20-21*

🌿 "Force (a betrothed damsel in the field) and lie with her." – *Deuteronomy 22:25*

Stoning appears to have been the most common form of execution, with "the edge of the sword" a close second and hanging third.

Among the Romans, of course, crucifixion was the favored mode of execution.

Quite a sacrifice

The largest sacrificial offering in the Bible occurs in 1 Kings 8:63, when Solomon dedicated his temple with the blood of "two and twenty thousand oxen, and an hundred and twenty thousand sheep."

Heavenly figures

In keeping with His majesty, God is attended to by a heavenly host of considerable size.

According to Psalms 68:17, "the chariots of God are twenty thousand," while Deuteronomy 33:2 says that he comes "with ten thousands of saints." Those saints, incidentally, are but a few of the "ten thousand times ten thousand, and thousands of thousands" to be found in heaven (Revelation 5:11).

Feast or famine

There are literally dozens of famines in the Bible, beginning with the one in Genesis 12:10 that sent Abraham to Egypt.

But there are also 13 great feasts, the first of which was hosted by Abraham on "the same day that (his son) Isaac was weaned" (Genesis 21:8).

In addition, there were two great birthday parties, the first thrown by the Egyptian Pharaoh for himself (Genesis 40:20-22), the second held by Herod (Matthew 14:6), where he gave Salome the head of John the Baptist, as she requested – her reward for dancing.

Picky eaters

One thing that wouldn't be found at very many Old Testament celebrations was food prepared from "anything that dieth of itself." According to Deuteronomy 14:21, "thou shalt give it unto the stranger that is in thy gates, that he may eat it; or thou mayest sell it unto an alien."

The same section warns that forbidden foods, however they are killed, include eagle, owl, pelican, camel, stork and bat.

By the pricking of my thumbs... something wicked this way comes!

How can you tell if someone is truly wicked? The Bible offers the following guidelines: They are as follows:

- 🌿 "Doth persecute the poor." – *Psalms 10:2*

- 🌿 "Boasteth of his heart's desire, and blesseth the covetous." – *Psalms 10:3*

- 🌿 "Bend their bow... that they may privily shoot at the upright in heart."
  – *Psalms 11:2*

- 🌿 "Walk on every side." – *Psalms 12:8*

- 🌿 "Oppress." – *Psalms 17:9*

- 🌿 "Plotteth against the just, and gnasheth upon him with his teeth." – *Psalms 37:12*

- 🌿 "(Draw) out the sword... to cast down the poor and needy." – *Psalms 37:14*

- 🌿 "Borroweth, and payeth not again."
  – *Psalms 37:21*

- 🌿 "Are estranged from the womb: They go astray as soon as they be born, speaking lies." – *Psalms 58:3*

- 🌿 "(Laid) a snare." – *Psalms 119:110*

The 12 tribes of Israel

The Hebrew tribes were established by the dozen sons of Jacob: Reuben, Issachar, Dan, Simeon, Zebulun, Naphtali, Levi, Joseph, Gad, Judah, Benjamin and Asher. However, tribes were also founded by two grandsons, Ephraim and Manasseh, but theirs usually counted as only one tribe.

But if there were 14 sons and grandsons, why do we refer to them as the 12 tribes?

Because the Levites were not given land. Rather, the members were charged with overseeing worship and were distributed among the other tribes.

Scholars who do count the Levites often discount Ephraim and Manasseh, grouping them with Jacob's tribe.

Where exactly is the "skin of your teeth"?

It's right outside of them, according to the Bible.

In Job 19:20, the prosperous Uzite is tortured by the devil: His donkeys and camels are stolen, his sheep are killed, his children die when a roof collapses, his body is covered with sores, and yet still he refuses to curse the Lord.

At one point, while recounting his endless torment, Job says, "My bone cleaveth to my skin and to my flesh, and I am escaped with the skin of my teeth."

In other words, Job has been left with just the little flesh that remains on his bones and face.

No one knows how or why, but the expression has changed over the years to "Escaped by the skin of my teeth." This saying suggests something quite different – that a person has barely escaped being nabbed, which isn't the same thing at all.

Famous last words

The Bible tells us that the last words spoken by some of its greatest figures are these:

Moses: "Happy art thou, O Israel: who is like unto thee, O people saved by the Lord, the shield of thy help, and who is the sword of thy excellency! and thine enemies shall be found liars unto thee; and thou shalt tread upon their high places" (Deuteronomy 33:29).

David, speaking to Solomon, left instructions about dealing with the dying king's enemy Shimei, the son of Gera, a Benjamite of Bahurim: "I swear to him by the Lord, saying, I will not put thee to death with the sword. Now therefore hold him not guiltless: For thou art a wise man, and knowest what thou oughtest to do unto him; but his hoar head bring thou down to the grave with blood."

Jesus, according to Luke 23:46, said from the cross, "Father, into thy hands I commend my spirit."

John 19:30 says he uttered, "It is finished."

Matthew and Mark both recount that Jesus cried out in a loud voice but said nothing else before dying.

Who's who among angels?

The hierarchy of angels was formalized by religious scholars in the 4th century, who based their rankings on the writings of Paul, among others (including Ephesians 1:21, Colossians 1:16, and others).

From the most powerful and hallowed, the rankings are:

First Hierarchy:
Seraphim
Cherubim
Thrones

Second Hierarchy:
Dominions
Principalities
Powers

Third Hierarchy:
Virtues
Archangels
Angels

Who's who among the devils?

Just as there are hierarchies above, so there are levels for their fallen kinfolk, the devils.

One of history's most famous exorcists, Father Sebastien Michaelis, described the ranking of devils in his *Admirable History* (1612). He also noted the sins of which each devil is in charge:

The Devil: Lucifer

First Hierarchy:
Beelzebub (pride)
Leviathan (sins "directly repugnant unto faith")
Asmodeus (luxuriousness and wantonness)
Balberith (homicides, quarrels, blasphemy)
Astaroth (idleness and sloth)
Verrine (impatience)
Gressil (impurity and uncleanliness)
Sonneillon (hatred)

Second Hierarchy:
Carreau (hardheartedness)
Carnivean (obscenity)
Oeillet (temptation to "break the vow of poverty")
Rosier (causes people to fall hopelessly in love, turning them from God or from their spouses)
Verrier (disobedience)

Third Hierarchy:
Belias (arrogance)
Olivier (mercilessness toward the poor)
Iuvart (various)

Friar Francesco Mario Guazzo, in his *Compendium Maleficarum* (1608), concentrated not on devils but on their servants, or demons. He identified six kinds. From the most powerful to the least powerful they are:

Fire devils, who live in the upper air and help to supervise the other five groups.

Aerial Devils, who inhabit the air around us and have the most direct access to us.

Terrestrial devils, who dwell in the woods, fields and forests.

Aqueous devils, who reside in rivers, lakes and seas.

Subterranean devils, who abide in caves and underground.

Heliophobic devils, who hate the light and only move about at night.

The most feared figure in the Bible

Despite the fact that the antichrist is despised beyond measure, he is only mentioned in John – and there, just four times:

"Little children, it is the last time: And as ye have heard that antichrist shall come, even now are there many antichrists; whereby we know that it is the last time." – *1 John 2:18*

"He is antichrist, that denieth the Father and the Son." – *1 John 2:22*

"And every spirit that confesseth not that Jesus Christ is come in the flesh is not of God: And this is that spirit of antichrist, whereof ye have heard that it should come; and even now already is it in the world." – *1 John 4:3*

"For many deceivers are entered into the world, who confess not that Jesus Christ is come in the flesh. This is a deceiver and an antichrist." – *2 John 7*

Which is it?

Alas, we'll never know which of these accounts in the Bible is accurate.

In 1 Samuel 31:4-6, we are told that Saul "took a sword and fell upon it." Just a few lines later, in 2 Samuel 1:10, a man tells David that Saul asked the stranger to slay him, and "so I stood upon him, and slew him." Most scholars seem to feel that the young man lied to the king, perhaps to win his favor at slaying his enemy.

In Matthew 27:5, we are informed that Judas "hanged himself" after betraying Jesus. Yet Acts 1:18 says that he threw himself down into a field and "burst asunder in the midst, and all his bowels gushed out." Tradition has it that Matthew's account is correct.

Moderation...and then some

In Numbers 6:3, we're told that the Nazarites refrained from drinking wine, which is admirable enough. But they may have carried their teetotaling a bit too far, for the Bible says that they also refused to "eat moist grapes, or dried."

Where did the Last Supper take place?

Though we will probably never know for certain, it is likely that the Last Supper was held in "a large upper room" (Luke 22:12) of the house of Mary, mother of the Apostle Mark (Acts 12:12).

This was also the place where the men gathered after the death of the Rabbi, and also

where Jesus was said to have met with them following his death and Resurrection.

The clever assassin

After the Moabites invaded Israel, the conquering King Eglon demanded crushing taxes from the Jews. Intent on freeing his people from the cruel reign, bold Ehud hid a knife beneath his clothing, lashed to his thigh. Claiming he had an important secret message for the king, he was granted an audience. A search by guards turned up no weapons – but they had only checked on his left side, unaware that Ehud was left-handed.

As soon as he was near the heavy king, Judges 3:21-22 tells us he "thrust it into his belly: And the shaft also went in after the blade; and the fat closed upon the blade so that he could not draw the dagger out of his belly."

Ehud was able to exit from the "summer parlor" in which they had met, since it was quite some time before the servants dared to open the closed doors.

What did Joseph's brothers hate even more than his coat?

They were jealous, of course, when their father, Jacob, gave the 17-year-old a "coat of many colors" (Genesis 37:3). After all, Joseph was Jacob's favorite, being his 11th son and "the son of his old age."

However, that wasn't what drove them to sell the boy into slavery. It was his dreams. Joseph told them that he dreamed "we were binding

sheaves in the field, and, lo, my sheaf arose, and then stood upright; and, behold, your sheaves stood round about, and made obeisance to my sheaf."

For this, says Genesis 37:8, "they hated him yet the more."

Hosea by any other name...

Some of the important Biblical names mean:

Abraham: *Father of multitudes*

Bathsheba: *Daughter of oath*

Benjamin: *Son of my right hand*

Daniel: *My judge is God*

David: *Beloved*

Elijah: *God is my salvation*

Ezekiel: *God gives strength*

Gabriel: *Man of God*

Hosea: *Salvation*

Isaac: *Laughter*

Jacob: *Supplants*

Jesus: *God of salvation*

Jonah: *Dove*

Mary: *Stubbornness*

Michael: *Who is like God?*

Noah: *Comfort*

Peter: *Rock*

Solomon: *Peaceable*

Dating the Old Testament

No original fragments of the first handwritten Bibles survive. We can only speculate about the ages of the books of the Bible, based on events it refers to and mentions of the books in other, contemporary texts.

The Five Books of Moses are believed to have been written between 1000 B.C. and 400 B.C. although, obviously, the stories were told orally for centuries before they were written down.

The writing of the books of Joshua, Judges, Ruth, Samuel and Kings overlapped the writing of the Five Books of Moses, occurring sometime around 600 B.C. These books are popularly known as the books of the Former Prophets, since they deal with the early history of Israel.

The books of the Latter Prophets are by authors who speak for God. These books, and the dates in which they were written, are: Isaiah (800-500 B.C.), Jeremiah (700-600 B.C.), Ezekiel (600 B.C.).

The books written by the "minor prophets" — Hosea, Joel, Obadiah, Amos, Micah, Nahum, Habakkuk, Zephaniah, Haggai, Zechariah and Malachi — were written around 600-500 B.C.

The dates of the books generally called the Writings are for the most part not known. Only Daniel can be dated, having been written around 200 B.C. The rest of the books in this grouping are Psalms, Proverbs, Job, Ecclesiastes, Chronicles, the Song of Solomon, Ruth, Lamentations, Esther, Ezra and Nehemiah.

The oldest copies of the Bibles are the fragments known as the Dead Sea Scrolls, which date as far back as 300 B.C.

Was something lost in the translation?

In Job 29:6, Job says that when he was a young man, "I washed my steps with butter."

That would make visitors slip and fall, of course. It is likely he meant he used some kind of polish to make them shine.

How many words are in the Bible?

There are nearly 774,000 words in all — a total of 66 books, 1,189 chapters and 31,173 verses. The exact center of the Bible can be found in Psalm 118:8.

When were the Gospels written?

As far as can be determined from events mentioned in the text itself, Mark was the first to be written. This was done circa 75 A.D.

Though it appears first in the New Testament, Matthew appears to have been written second, since it corrects certain grammatical errors in the other Gospel. The date of its writing is unknown.

Luke and John seem to have followed in that order though, once again, no one knows when they were written.

J.F.K. and Luke

In his inaugural address, President John F. Kennedy said the following: "For of those to whom much is given, much is required."

That's a slight variation of this from Luke 12:48: "For unto whomsoever much is given, of him shall be much required."

More common phrases from the Bible:

❦ "Am I my brother's keeper?" – *Genesis 4:9*

❦ "And ye shall eat the fat of the land." – *Genesis 45:18*

❦ "A man hath no better thing under the sun, than to eat, and to drink, and to be merry." – *Ecclesiastes 8:15*

❦ "Woe is me!" – *Isaiah 6:5*

❦ "Behold, the nations are as a drop of a bucket." – *Isaiah 40:15*

❦ "I am holier than thou." – *Isaiah 65:5*

❦ "Beware of false prophets, which come to you in sheep's clothing, but inwardly they are ravening wolves." – *Matthew 7:15*

❦ "He girded up his loins." – *1 Kings 18:46*

❦ "Set thine house in order." – *2 Kings 20:1*

Written in Stone

Parts of the Bible were literally written in stone, by the finger of God. But, figuratively speaking, all of it is written in stone. God is quite explicit about the sanctity of the words He's given us:

"What thing soever I command you, observe to do it: Thou shalt not add thereto, nor diminish from it." – *Deuteronomy 12:32*

"If any man shall add unto these things, God shall add unto him the plagues that are written in this book: And if any man shall take away from the words of the book of this prophecy, God shall take away his part out of the book of life, and out of the holy city, and from the things which are written in this book."

– Revelation 22:18-19

It's Greek to me

The Five Books of Moses – Genesis, Exodus, Leviticus, Numbers and Deuteronomy – are called the Pentateuch by Christians, from the Greek meaning five books.

To Jews, these books are known collectively as the Torah, from the Hebrew word for laws, because within the stories they tell, that is what they're really all about.

Did you know...

That the earliest Bibles, handwritten on scrolls, contained neither punctuation, verses nor chapters? These were added later to make it easier to read.

How, then, did scribes know that they hadn't left out a word or two? Because they had what were called "center words:" If a specific word did not show up where it was supposed to, the writer was forced to start again.

Let there be light
...and light

God creates day and night on the first day, in Genesis 1:4, yet it isn't until 1:14, the fourth day, that He creates "lights in the firmament of the heaven to divide the day from the night."

Is this an inconsistency? Not according to experts on the Bible. They say that the first light was the "greater" light, the sun, and the second light was the "lesser" light, the moon.

They were not referred to specifically, it is said, because their names are dangerously close to the words for the Babylonian sun and moon gods — references that the authors of the Bible would have wanted to avoid.

Why was Adam's home
called Eden?

Eden is the ancient Sumerian word for plain. Though that word doesn't exactly summon up visions of paradise, it must be remembered that the garden itself wasn't called Eden, but that "the Lord God planted a garden eastward in Eden" (Genesis 2:8).

The word "plain," however, does accurately describe the general region, believed to be in southeastern Iraq, in which the garden is thought to have been located.

How do we know where
the garden was?

We have a pretty good idea because the Bible identifies a river in the garden that "parted and

became into four heads" (Genesis 2:10): Pishon, Gihon, Tigris and Euphrates. That location could only be ancient Babylonia, now modern Iraq.

Why was the first man called Adam?

In Hebrew, the name means man or mankind. When God brought Adam to life, he was bringing all humans to life.

The name appears to have been derived from the word *adamah* which means ground or dust – which, of course, is what God used to create Adam.

Both words come from the root *adom* meaning red, like the color of the clay from which Adam was made.

Why was the first woman called Eve?

There is some dispute as to the origin of the name. Many scholars believe it comes from the Hebrew *havah*, which means life.

However, other scholars maintain it derives from the Sumerian word *ev,* which meant rib.

Who was the original doubting Thomas?

He was Thomas of John 20:24-29, who did not believe that the disciples had seen the resurrected Jesus – and refused to believe so "except I shall see in his hands the print of the nails, and put my finger into the print of the nails, and thrust my hand into his side."

Eight days later, Jesus came to his disciples again and said, "Thomas, reach hither thy finger, and behold my hands; and reach hither thy hand, and thrust it into my side: And be not faithless, but believing."

And Thomas doubted no more!

Nobody's fool

According to the Bible, someone is a fool if he or she does the following things:

- "(Says) in his heart, There is no God. They are corrupt, they have done abominable works." – *Psalms 14:1*

- "(Are) clamorous...simple, and knoweth nothing." – *Proverbs 9:13*

- "Hideth hatred with lying lips, and... uttereth a slander." – *Proverbs 10:18*

- "(Thinks) it is as sport...to do mischief." – *Proverbs 10:23*

- "Make a mock at sin." – *Proverbs 14:9*

- "Rageth, and is confident." – *Proverbs 14:16*

- "Despiseth his father's instructions." – *Proverbs 15:5*

- "Despiseth his mother." – *Proverbs 15:20*

- "Hath no delight in understanding." – *Proverbs 18:2*

- "Enter into contention." – *Proverbs 18:6*

🐛 "(Is) meddling." – *Proverbs 20:3*

🐛 "Uttereth all his mind." – *Proverbs 29:11*

🐛 "Walketh in darkness." – *Ecclesiastes 2:14*

🐛 "Foldeth his hands together, and eateth his own flesh." – *Ecclesiastes 4:5*

According to God, the practitioner of all these things, the "prating fool shall fall" – an understatement indeed! – *Proverbs 10:8*

Where in the Bible are we warned about the "forbidden fruit"?

Nowhere.

The phrase came about much later to describe the apple Adam and Eve tasted in the Garden of Eden.

The exact words used to describe the fruit and its tree in Genesis are these:

"But of the tree of the knowledge of good and evil, thou shalt not eat of it; for in the day that thou eatest thereof thou shalt surely die" (2:17).

And:

"But of the fruit of the tree which is in the midst of the garden, God hath said, Ye shall not eat of it, neither shall ye touch it, lest ye die" (3:3).

The landmark of Cain

After slaying his brother, Cain "dwelt in the land of Nod" (Genesis 4:16) where he had a son. (The Bible does not tell us who or from where Cain's wife came.)

The last act of Cain recorded in the Bible is his building of the city of Enoch, which he named after his son (4:17).

Other titles inspired by the Bible:

In addition to Ernest Hemingway, mentioned earlier, other authors and filmmakers have used the Bible to provide titles for their works. For example:

For his novel of two brothers and their rivalry, John Steinbeck dipped into Genesis 4:16 for *East of Eden*.

The film for which Sidney Poitier won an Oscar, about a handyman who helps build a chapel, took its name from Matthew 6:28: *Lilies of the Field*.

Director Ingmar Bergman's film *Through a Glass, Darkly* is from 1 Corinthians 13:12.

The great cult novel of the 1960s by Robert A. Heinlein, about a messianic figure from Mars, borrowed its title from Exodus 2:22: Describing his flight from Egypt and arrival in Midian, Moses calls himself a *Stranger in a Strange Land*.

The classic film *The Way of All Flesh* also got its name from the Bible, though from a very specific edition. The original line in Joshua 23:14 is, "I am going the way of all the earth." The substitution of "flesh" for "earth" came about with the publication of the English Catholic Bible in 1609.

It was Oliver Wendell Holmes, not Jesus

In Matthew 5:39, Jesus does advise his followers, "But I say unto you, That ye resist not evil: But whosoever shall smite thee on thy right cheek, turn to him the other also."

Luke 6:29 quotes it thusly: "And unto him that smiteth thee on the one cheek offer also the other."

So where did we get the words "turn the other cheek"? That came from the poem *Non Resistance*, in which author Holmes wrote:

> *"Wisdom has taught us to be calm and meek,*
> *To take one blow, and turn the other cheek.*
> *It is not written what a man shall do*
> *If the rude caitiff smite the other too!"*

The second oldest man in the Bible

Everybody seems to know that Methuselah – whose name in Hebrew means "Man of the Javelin" – lived to be 969 years old. But few seem to know that the next-oldest man in the Bible came close to that: And it was none other than Methuselah's grandfather, Jared. According to Genesis 5:18-19, he lived a long 962 years.

Noah died at the age of 950. After his death, the longest-lived figures in the Bible tended to be in their 120s.

Who were the "giants"?

Genesis 6:4 clearly states that a very different breed of creature once dwelt with humans upon the earth:

"There were giants in the earth in those days...when the sons of God came in unto the daughters of men, and they bare children to them, the same became mighty men which were of old, men of renown."

Whoever these demigods and titans were, they were destroyed in the flood – though some scholars speculate that Goliath and his giant kin were throwbacks to those beings.

Step by step

Jacob had a dream.

And Genesis 28:12 tells us that in his dream, he beheld "a ladder set up on the earth, and the top of it reached to heaven: And behold the angels of God ascending and descending on it."

But was it, strictly speaking, a ladder that he saw?

Not likely. The word *sullam* actually means a ramp or staircase – perhaps like those that were commonly found around the aforementioned ziggurats. It was the King James version of the Bible that gave us the ladder – though why and how are not known.

"Let my people go"

This very famous line from Exodus 5:1, one of the most famous from the Old Testament, is widely thought to have been uttered by Moses to Pharaoh.

Not so.

When God told Moses to go back to Egypt and free the Hebrew slaves, Moses rejoined, "O my Lord, I am not eloquent, neither heretofore, nor since thou hast spoken unto thy servant: But I am slow of speech, and of a slow tongue" (Exodus 4:10).

God was displeased, and said that Moses'

brother Aaron should go with him and do the talking for him.

Thus, it was Aaron who stood at Moses' side "and told Pharaoh, Thus saith the Lord God of Israel, Let my people go."

Who was the first to heap mischief on another?

It was God Himself. At least, that's what He threatened.

In Deuteronomy 32:22-23, the Jews are warned never to incur God's wrath: "For a fire is kindled in mine anger, and shall burn unto the lowest hell, and shall consume the earth with her increase, and set on fire the foundations of the mountains.

"I will heap mischiefs upon them; I will spend mine arrows upon them."

Obviously, Biblical "mischief" is somewhat more severe than the impish behavior the term implies today.

"What hath God wrought!"

The line was the first one to be sent by telegraph, dispatched by Samuel Morse on May 24, 1844.

It was not coined by the inventor, however: It is from Numbers 23:23:

"Surely there is no enchantment against Jacob, neither is there any divination against Israel: According to this time it shall be said of Jacob and of Israel, What hath God wrought!"

Exactly when did the events in the Old Testament occur?

Since it's difficult to keep track of who did what and when, here's a general time frame. Note that there are no historical dates corresponding to Adam and Eve and to the Flood, so we begin with –

Abraham, Isaac, and Jacob in Canaan:
Circa 1800-1700 B.C.

The Israelites in Egypt:
Circa 1700-1250 B.C.

The Conquest of the Promised Land:
Circa 1220-1200 B.C.

Philistines settle on the coast of Palestine and make war with the Jews:
Circa 1150 B.C.

The Story of Ruth:
Circa 1100 B.C.

The Reign of Saul:
Circa 1030-1010 B.C.

The Reign of David:
Circa 1010-970 B.C.

The Reign of Solomon:
Circa 970-931 B.C.

The Time of the Two Kingdoms of Israel and Judah:
931-587 B.C.

Following the fall of Jerusalem in 587 B.C., the Jews were in exile. They lived under Alexander the Great and then a string of Ptolemies until 197 B.C., after which a succession of tyrants endeavored to oppress them.

Thanks largely to the efforts of the warrior priests, the Maccabees, beginning in 166 B.C., the land of Judea became autonomous in 142 and remained so until Pompey conquered the region in 63 B.C.

This began the period of Roman control of the Holy Land – the reign into which Jesus was born.

The flesh pot that isn't a fleshpot

As used in the Bible, the term "flesh pot" isn't quite what we take it to mean today.

Exodus 16:3 quotes the unhappy Hebrews in the wilderness grumbling, "Would to God we had died by the hand of the Lord in the land of Egypt, when we sat by the flesh pots, and when we did eat bread to the full."

The current usage of fleshpot means decadent comfort, with all of our physical needs cared for. In the time of Moses, however, it was a large caldron that was used to boil meat.

Is there such a thing as a straight and narrow path?

Not in the Bible, anyway.

In Matthew 7:13-14, the entire phrase is as follows: "Enter ye in at the strait gate: For wide is the gate, and broad is the way, that leadeth to destruction, and many there be which go in thereat.

"Because strait is the gate, and narrow is the way, which leadeth unto life, and few there be that find it."

Strait, in this context, means narrow, which makes the expression a bit redundant – though Jesus wanted to emphasize that the way to salvation is the tougher one to negotiate.

What became of the Golden Calf?

Thanks to Cecil B. DeMille and his wonderful film *The Ten Commandments*, many people have this vision of Moses throwing the tablets of the Ten Commandments at the Golden Calf, and the earth swallowing it up.

That isn't what happened, however.

After "he cast the tables out of his hands, and brake them" (Exodus 32:19) at the foot of Mt. Sinai, Moses "took the calf which they had made, and burnt it in the fire, and ground it to powder, and strawed it upon the water, and made the children of Israel drink of it" (32:20). After that, he ordered those who were still loyal to God to slay those who had sinned: Three thousand Israelites were killed.

Who was the world's first scapegoat?

Leviticus 16:7-10 tells of how Aaron took two goats and presented "them before the Lord at the door of the tabernacle of the congregation.

"And Aaron shall cast lots upon the two goats; one lot for the Lord, and the other for the scapegoat.

"And Aaron shall bring the goat upon which the Lord's lot fell, and offer him for a sin offering.

"But the goat, on which the lot fell to be the scapegoat, shall be presented alive before the Lord, to make an atonement with him, and to let him go for a scapegoat into the wilderness."

The passage suggests that though one goat dies and the other lives, the one sent into the wilderness is the less fortunate: For that goat is the one which carries with it the sins of the people. In other words, though they have sinned, it's the scapegoat that gets the punishment.

Who was the first person to put words in someone's mouth?

It was King David's nephew Joab, commander in chief of Israel's army

Hoping to bring David and his wayward son Absalom together again, Joab sends an unnamed woman to see David reportedly with an apology from his son.

As 2 Samuel 14:2-3 tells it, "Joab sent to Tekoah, and fetched thence a wise woman, and said unto her, I pray thee, feign thyself to be a mourner, and put on now mourning apparel, and anoint not thyself with oil, but be as a woman that had a long time mourned for the dead:

"And come to the king, and speak on this manner unto him. So Joab put the words in her mouth."

And who is the original man after his own heart?

As the last of the Judges, it was Samuel's right to authorize any and all burnt offerings. When Saul does so without permission, in the midst of battling the Philistines, Samuel scolds and warns him in 1 Samuel 13:13-14:

"Thou hast done foolishly; thou has not kept the commandment of the Lord thy God, which he commanded thee: for now would the Lord have established thy kingdom upon Israel forever.

"But now thy kingdom shall not continue: The Lord hath sought him a man after his own heart."

The man in question was David, who would ultimately triumph over Saul.

What was the first thorn in someone's side?

They were the Canaanites. God had instructed Moses and his people to drive them out (along with their evil gods) as soon as they reached the Promised Land.

As it says in Numbers 33:55, "If ye will not drive out the inhabitants of the land from before you; then it shall come to pass, that those which ye let remain of them shall be pricks in your eyes, and thorns in your sides, and shall vex you in the land wherein ye dwell."

Did you know...

The word "gospel" comes from the Old English word for "good news," which comes from the Greek word *evangelion*. The latter word, of course, is the root of the word "evangelists."

And did you also know...

When Jesus referred to the attendees at the Sermon on the Mount as "the salt of the earth"

(Matthew 5:13), he wasn't comparing them to the flavorful condiment.

Rather, he was referring to the use of salt as a preservative. In other words, those who are free of sin and hate are the ones who will preserve the earth.

The first double-edged sword wasn't a sword at all

In Proverbs, a father is telling his son to beware the temptations of a loose woman.

For, as he says in 5:4-6, "Her end is bitter as wormwood, sharp as a two-edged sword. Her feet go down to death; her steps take hold on hell. Lest thou shouldest ponder the path of life, her ways are moveable, that thou canst not know them."

As it happens, the Biblical two-edged sword isn't anything like the two-edged sword we refer to today. The father meant that the "sword" (or loose woman) will cut his son coming and going. Today, a two-edged sword is a person who does both good and bad.

Who was the first lamb to the slaughter?

No one knows, though we do know it was a holy person whose task it was to bring the chosen people back to Zion. And for doing so, this holy person nobly suffered for the sins of others.

As it is expressed in Isaiah 53:6-7, "All we like sheep have gone astray; we have turned every one to his own way; and the Lord hath laid on him the iniquity of us all.

"He was oppressed, and he was afflicted, yet he opened not his mouth: He is brought as a lamb to the slaughter, and as a sheep before her shearers is dumb, so he openeth not his mouth."

What sets a person's teeth on edge?

We are informed, in Jeremiah 31:30, that "Every man that eateth the sour grape, his teeth shall be set on edge."

In other words, metaphorically speaking, if you sin, you'll have to suffer the consequences.

No one is quite sure what having "teeth on edge" means, though in the context it suggests that they come together edge-to-edge, as when one sucks a lemon or hears chalk scraping on a blackboard.

What does it mean to have feet of clay?

Actually, it was not a person who had clay feet, but a kingdom – figuratively speaking.

In Daniel 2:31-33, we read about a statue seen by King Nebuchadnezzar in a dream: "This great image, whose brightness was excellent, stood before thee; and the form thereof was terrible.

"This image's head was of fine gold, his breast and his arms of silver, his belly and his thighs of brass.

"His legs of iron, his feet part of iron and part of clay."

The image stood for successively weaker kingdoms: Babylon at the time, Median next, then

Persia. At the bottom was the weakened Macedonian empire – part of it iron and part of it clay.

Is it old wine in new bottles or new wine in old bottles?

It's "neither do men put new wine into old bottles" in Matthew 9:17 – though old wine in new bottles is a misquote many people use.

Truth be told, though, the translation is probably incorrect in either case: The world in which Jesus moved did not use wine bottles at all, but wine skins.

What "fell by the wayside" in the Bible?

It was seeds that fell, when the sower went forth to sow. As Jesus says in Matthew 13:4, "And when he sowed, some of the seeds fell by the wayside, and the fowls came and devoured them up."

Of course, Jesus is not really talking about seeds but about his own teachings: Although he realizes that some of his own seeds (lessons) will not fall on fertile ground, he urges, "Who hath ears to hear, let him hear" (13:9).

To whom was Jesus referring when He spoke of the blind leading the blind?

The Pharisees – the ancient Jewish sect with whom he had serious ideological differences.

In Matthew 15:12-14, it says, "Then came his

disciples, and said unto him, Knowest thou that the Pharisees were offended, after they heard this saying?

"But he answered and said, Every plant, which my heavenly Father hath not planted, shall be rooted up.

"Let them alone: They be blind leaders of the blind. And if the blind lead the blind, both shall fall into the ditch."

What was it that the Lord gave and took away?

It was everything poor, oppressed Job owned.

Tearing his clothes and shaving his head, the despairing Job falls to the ground and says in Job 1:21, "Naked came I out of my mother's womb, and naked shall I return thither: The Lord gave, and the Lord hath taken away."

The phrase, "The Lord giveth and the Lord taketh away" is not found in any Biblical text.

A final sample of Bible sayings...

❧ "They that take the sword shall perish with the sword." – *Matthew 26:52*

❧ "It is more blessed to give than to receive." – *Acts 20:35*

❧ "The powers that be." – *Romans 13:1*

❧ "In the twinkling of an eye."
   – *1 Corinthians 15:52*

❧ "O death, where is thy sting?"
   – *1 Corinthians 15:55*

🦋 "Ye suffer fools gladly." – *2 Corinthians 11:19*

🦋 "(A) labor of love." – *1 Thessalonians 1:3*

🦋 "Fight the good fight." – *1 Timothy 6:12*

The expression "God save the King" is also from the Bible. In 1 Samuel 10:24 it is written, "And Samuel said to all the people, See ye him whom the Lord hath chosen, that there is none like him among all the people? And all the people shouted, and said, God save the King."

Another Biblical phrase that has undergone a few changes is "a fly in the ointment." In its original version, in Ecclesiastes 10:1, it says, "Dead flies cause the ointment of the apothecary to send forth a stinking savour." The two phrases mean more or less the same thing, though the rephrasing is a lot less graphic.

Finally, this phrase from Matthew 6:3 has taken a totally different meaning than what was intended: "Let not thy left hand know what thy right hand doeth." Jesus was speaking of discreetly and quietly giving money to a worthy cause while not letting others know. For if the "private you" gives to charity, and the "public you" promotes that fact, is it goodness – or self-promotion?

Today, of course, for the left hand to not know what the right hand is doing signifies an unwelcome state of confusion.

Who were the first people to fall from grace?

They were converts to Christianity who insisted on following certain aspects of the traditional Mosaic Law.

It was Paul's intent to show people that Christians were bound to God by faith, not rituals – in this case, circumcision. As he put it in Galatians 5:2-4, "I Paul say unto you, that if ye be circumcised, Christ shall profit you nothing.

"For I testify again to every man that is circumcised, that he is a debtor to the whole law.

"Christ is become of no effect unto you, whosoever of you are justified by the law; ye are fallen from grace."

What in the Bible is "clear as crystal"?

It's "a pure river of water of life, clear as crystal, proceeding out of the throne of God and of the Lamb" (Revelation 22:1).

Where are the Biblical "Four corners of the Earth"?

Isaiah first referred to them (11:12), and they appear again in Revelation 7:1.

Not everyone believed that the Earth was flat, even in the time of Isaiah. Thus, the four corners are taken to mean the four directions: north, south, east and west.

More names and their meanings...

Adlai: *God's justice*

Ahab: *Father's brother*

Bela: *Destroying*

Caleb: *Dog*

Deborah: *Bee*

Gomer: *Ember*

Hannah: *Grace*

Immanuel: *God is with us*

Ishmael: *God hears*

Jeremiah: *God will elevate*

Jezebel: *Chaste*

Jonathan: *Given by God*

Joseph: *May God add children*

Nathan: *He gave*

Ophrah: *Faun*

Rachel: *Ewe*

Ruth: *Beloved*

Who is the least perceptive man in the Bible?

That would have to be the Pharisee Nicodemus.

In John 3:1-7, we are told that he came to Jesus by night and said to him, "Rabbi, we know that thou art a teacher come from God: For no man can do these miracles that thou doest, except God be with you."

Jesus answered, "Verily, verily, I say unto thee, except a man be born again, he cannot see the kingdom of God."

One can almost imagine Nicodemus scratching his head as he asks, "How can a man be born when he is old? Can he enter the second time into his mother's womb, and be born?"

Jesus answered patiently, "Verily, verily, I say

unto thee, Except a man be born of water and of the Spirit, he cannot enter the kingdom of God. That which is born of the flesh is flesh; and that which is born of the Spirit is spirit. Marvel not that I said unto thee, Ye must be born again."

What is the first war
mentioned in the Bible?

Violent creatures that we are, it happens relatively quickly: In Genesis 14:1-2 we learn, "And it came to pass in the days of Amraphel king of Shinar, Arioch king of Ellasar, Chedorlaomer king of Elam, and Tidal king of nations; that these made war with Bera king of Sodom, and with Birsha king of Gomorrah, Shinab king of Admah, and Shemeber king of Zeboiim, and the king of Bela, which is Zoar."

It was a violent war known as the War of the Kings of the North and appears to have taken place around 2000 B.C.

What is the most frequently
used name for Jesus?

It is Son of Man, which appears 82 times in the New Testament – 81 times in the Gospels, and once in Acts.

The name Son of Man first appears in the Old Testament, in Daniel 7:13, as a messianic prophecy: "I saw in the night visions, and, behold, one like the Son of Man came with the clouds of heaven."

Son of Man is taken to signify the humanity of Jesus, as opposed to Son of God, which refers to his divinity.

What are the other names of Jesus?

Jesus is called by 154 other names in the New Testament, including these:

The Advocate – *John 2:1*

Alpha and Omega – *Revelation 1:8, 22:13*

The Bridegroom – *John 3:29*

The Chief Shepherd – *1 Peter 5:4*

The Chosen One – *Luke 23:35*

The Eldest of Many Brothers – *Romans 8:29*

The First and the Last – *Revelation 1:17, 2:8*

Firstborn of All Creation – *Colossians 1:15*

Glory – *John 12:41*

God of Glory – *Acts 7:2*

Greater Covenant – *Hebrews 7:22*

Head of Every Man – *1 Corinthians 11:3*

Hidden Manna – *Revelation 2:17*

Hope – *1 Timothy 1:2*

Image of the Unseen God – *Colossians 1:15*

Inexpressible Gift – *2 Corinthians 9:15*

Israel's Comforting – *Luke 2:25*

King of Kings – *Revelation 17:14, 1 Timothy 6:15*

Lamb Without Spot or Stain – *1 Peter 1:19*

Last Adam – *1 Corinthians 15:45*

Light of the World – *John 8:12*

Lion of the Tribe of Judah – *Revelation 5:5*

Living Bread – *John 6:51*

Lord of All Men – *Acts 10:36*

Main Cornerstone – *Ephesians 2:20*

The Man – *John 19:5*

Morning Star – *2 Peter 1:19, Revelation 2:28*

Only Son of the Father – *John 1:14*

Perfect Copy (of God's nature) – *Hebrews 1:3*

Power for Salvation – *Luke 1:69*

Precious Cornerstone – *1 Peter 2:6*

Prince of Life – *Acts 3:15*

Radiant Light of God's Glory – *Hebrews 1:3*

Righteous Judge – *2 Timothy 4:8*

Rising Sun – *Luke 1:78*

Ruler of All – *1 Timothy 6:15*

Second Adam – *Romans 5:12-21*

Son of the Blessed One – *Mark 14:61*

Spiritual Rock – *1 Corinthians 10:4*

True Vine – *John 15:1*

The Way – *John 14:6*

Word Was Made Flesh – *John 1:14*

Solomon the wise, Solomon the jealous

He was a great and wise king, but Solomon was also suspicious of those around him. And it would seem, his suspicions were justified.

Still, he may have gone a bit too far when King David died. David's nurse was the beautiful young Shunammite woman, Abishag: Upon his death,

David's son Adonijah asked for Solomon's permission to marry her. Instead, Solomon had the man slain, fearing that the offspring of such a marriage might one day threaten his throne.

The story is told in 1 Kings 2.

Did you know...

That Moses was the youngest of three children? His sister Miriam was the eldest child of Amram and Jochebed, and Aaron was the middle child.

Whose temple did Samson destroy?

It was constructed to honor Dagon, a Philistine god of the sea who was also worshiped as a god of corn.

As a point of interest, Samson is the anglicized version of the hero's name: His Hebrew name was Shimshon, "man of the sun."

How did Jehoshaphat, the fourth king of Judah, get his odd nickname?

Jehoshaphat reigned from 870-848 B.C. It is believed he came to be known as "Jumping Jehoshaphat" when he threw a fit after a fleet he ordered constructed (1 Kings 22:48) was lost in the Gulf of Akaba.

Words of wisdom from the Bible...

We've reminded you of some of the best known phrases from the Bible. However, some of the lesser known words are just as wise. For example:

🐦 "Whatsoever thy hand findeth to do, do it with thy might." – *Ecclesiastes 9:10*

🐦 "He that loveth his wife loveth himself." – *Ephesians 5:28*

🐦 "The words of wise men are heard in quiet more than the cry of him that ruleth among fools." – *Ecclesiastes 9:17*

🐦 "Lying lips are abomination to the Lord: But they that deal truly are his delight." – *Proverbs 12:22*

🐦 "Man that is born of a woman is of few days, and full of trouble." – *Job 14:1*

🐦 "A broken spirit drieth the bones." – *Proverbs 17:22*

🐦 "The wicked flee when no man pursueth." – *Proverbs 28:1*

🐦 "Neglect not the gift that is in thee." – *1 Timothy 4:14*

What's a Dodo and what does it mean?

In the Bible, the three men named Dodo were all good, intelligent men. The name itself means "loving."

Unfortunately, the name was also given to the clumsy, flightless birds of the islands of Mauritius and Reunion. Though the bird is now extinct, the name lives on suggesting a clumsy person and not the bold figures of the Bible!

How did Mary, Mother of Jesus, pass from life?

The scholar Epiphanius (315-403 A.D.) made a careful study of all surviving documents at the time, and concluded, "Nobody knows how she departed this world."

Her death is a fact largely accepted by the Church, though Catholic scholars point out that because she was free of sin, she may not have been subject to the same laws of mortality as other people.

One-hit wonders...

It's surprising how many common words are mentioned just once in the Bible – especially when a relatively specific word like "napkin" gets three mentions – *Luke 19:20, John 11:44 and John 20:7.*

Among these tough-to-find words in both the Old and New Testaments are:

Amounting – *2 Chronicles 3:8*
– yet amount isn't mentioned at all!

Belch – *Psalms 59:7*
– a surprise, since belching was considered a polite show of respect to one's host after being served a meal.

Castaway – *1 Corinthians 9:27*

Debase – *Isaiah 57:9*

Empire – *Esther 1:20*

Farm – *Matthew 22:5*

Grease – *Psalms 119:70*

Handwriting – *Colossians 2:14*

Industrious – *1 Kings 11:28*

Jewish – *Titus 1:14*

Kicked – *Deuteronomy 32:15*

Lavish – *Isaiah 46:6*

Mansions – *John 14:2*

Native – *Jeremiah 22:10*

Obscure – *Proverbs 20:20*

Parchments – *2 Timothy 4:13*

Quivered – *Habakkuk 3:16*

Reigning – *1 Samuel 16:1*

Sadness – *Ecclesiastes 7:3*

Taverns – *Acts 28:15*

Unclothed – *2 Corinthians 5:4*

Vein – *Job 28:1*

Wedlock – *Ezekiel 16:38*

Yell – *Jeremiah 51:38*

By the way, there are no words or names in the Bible that begin with "X."

Who was the first person to be called a Hebrew?

Though the Old Testament is the early history of the Jewish people, the word Hebrew does not appear until Genesis 14:13, "And there came one that had escaped, and told Abram the Hebrew."

It's both sad and ironic that the act of war is mentioned in the Bible before this important account of religion is ever mentioned!

The Nun who was not a nun...

Though there was a distinguished Nun in the Bible, the father of Joshua, his name is unrelated to the Christian word "nun."

The name of Nun comes from the Hebrew word for fish.

The word "nun" comes from the Latin *nonna,* the feminine form of *nonnus* or monk.

God's contract with the animals... signed with a rainbow!

When the Flood ended and Noah was able to leave the Ark, God made a covenant not just with him, but with "every living creature that is with you, of the fowl, of the cattle, and of every beast of the Earth with you; from all that come out of the Ark, every beast of the Earth" (Genesis 9:10). Truly, God was being noble and loving with all survivors, great and small.

The covenant was expressed in the lines that followed: God promised to cause no more floods, and he also "set my bow in the cloud" – the rainbow, which became the tangible "token of the covenant which I make between me and the earth" (Genesis 9:13).

In what year was Jesus born?

In the fifth century A.D., Dionysius Exiguus devised the designation *Anno Domini,* Latin for "in the year of our Lord," to describe the years after the birth of Jesus.

However, modern scholars believe that Dionysius' calculations may have been off.

Based on references to contemporary events in the Bible – such as the death of Herod the Great (Matthew 2:19) in 4 B.C., and the great taxation leveled by Cyrenius (Luke 2:1-2) – many researchers think that Jesus was actually born between 7 and 4 B.C.

What was the language of Jesus?

It was Aramaic, named after Aram, a country in southwestern Asia.

It was the daily language of Syria, Mesopotamia and Palestine, and was spoken by the Jews both during and following the Babylonian Exile (606-536 B.C.). It was the language of both Jesus and his Apostles.

What do we know of Barabbas?

It was the practice of the Romans to offer a Passover pardon to one prisoner. Pontius Pilate, the Roman procurator, offered the crowd freedom for Jesus or Barabbas: They chose Barabbas.

Little is known about the historical figure, save that he was "a robber" (John 18:40) and "a man who had been thrown into prison for an insurrection started in the city, and for murder" (Luke 23:19).

Historians suspect that Barabbas was a member of the Sicarii – "dagger men" or guerrillas who were devoted to overthrowing the Roman occupation. If so, he would have had many followers and very vocal allies in the crowd – which would account for his release.

Nothing of Barabbas' later life is known. But Swedish author Par Lagerkvist wrote a fictionalized account that was made into the movie starring Anthony Quinn.

The name Barabbas is Greek, from the Hebrew words for "son of a father."

Where did he come from?

Judas Iscariot is the only Apostle who did not come from Galilee.

He was from Kerioth, a town in southern Judea. Indeed, his name may tell us that: "Ish" means man, making him a man of Kerioth – Judas Ishkerioth. However, some scholars debate this interpretation of his name: They say that, like Barabbas, he may at one point have been a member of the Sicarii – the rebellious "dagger men." That would make him a man of the Sicarri – or "Ish Sicarri."

Judas' specialty was managing money, and he was in charge of the common fund of the Apostles (John 13:29).

Why is it called a papal bull?

The most reverent and important form of papal letter has nothing to do with the animal. Rather, the word comes from the Latin *bulla* – a heavy, round seal affixed to the document.

What exactly is in the Dead Sea Scrolls?

The collection of manuscripts and fragments was found by a shepherd in 1947 at the site of an ancient Qumran settlement.

The major texts are a set of rules for a community of monks: The Manual of Discipline, A Zadokite Document (a copy of which had been discovered previously in Cairo), and A Formulary of Blessings; two sets of hymns; commentaries on the Books of Micah, Nahum and Habakkuk; a lengthy discourse on Moses; the epic tale The War of the Sons of Light and the Sons of Darkness; and a guide for the Messianic Banquet, a future congregation of Israel.

Researchers believe that the scrolls were written between 170 B.C. and 68 A.D.

Where in the Bible is the book known as Koheleth?

It's the Hebrew name for Ecclesiastes and it means "the Preacher."

Ecclesiastes itself comes from the Greek word for preacher, *ekklesiastes.*

Why did Jesus utter the name "Eli" on the Cross?

When Jesus said "Eli, Eli, lama sabachthani" (Matthew 27:46), he was using a form of the Hebrew word *Elohim.* Elohim was the most commonly used word for God.

Jesus, of course, was asking God why He had forsaken him.

Where in the Bible is a Messiah first prophesied?

In Genesis 49. There, Jacob predicts that it is the tribe of Judah from which a Shiloh, messiah, or "anointed one," will spring (49:10 12).

The Greek word for Messiah is, of course, *Christos.*

Who was Leviticus?

It wasn't a "who," *per se*: The title of the third book of the Bible derives from the rites of the members of the tribe of Levi.

The chapters deal with the rites of sacrifice (1-7), the installation of priests (8-10), the laws of purity (11-16), the law of holiness (17-22), religious institutions (23-25), and blessings and curses (26).

Why isn't the Apocryhpha part of the Bible?

The Apocryhpha is the name given to 15 Jewish books, or segments of books, that were written between 200 B.C. and 100 A.D.

While the Hebrew leaders did not doubt the truths that these books contain, they did not feel that these books were the word of God – though most of the writings are accepted as part of the Greek Bible (Septuagint) and the Latin (Vulgate) Bible. The Apocryhpha contains the following writings:

The First Book of Esdras: largely comprised

of rewritten sections of Chronicles, Ezra and Nehemiah.

The Second Book of Esdras: seven visions said to be those of Ezra.

Tobit: the story of a blind Jewish boy whose sight is restored.

Judith: the story of a patriotic Jewish widow who fights the Assyrians.

The Book of Esther: six additional passages.

The Wisdom of Solomon: a collection of Hebrew wisdom.

Ecclesiasticus, the Wisdom of Jesus the Son of Sirach: all about the Hebrew way of life.

Baruch: prophesies regarding the future of the Jewish exiles.

The Letter of Jeremiah: a missive against idolatry.

The Prayer of Azariah and the Song of the Three Young Men: additions to Daniel.

Susanna: the story of the wife of a Jew who spurns the advances of two other men.

Bel and the Dragon: stories against idolatry.

The Prayer of Manasseh: a psalm of penitence.

The First Book of the Maccabees: the saga of the revolt of the Maccabees against the Seleucids, covering 175-35 B.C.

The Second Book of Maccabees: a different telling of the same story, covering 175-61 B.C.

Why is a book of the Bible called Numbers?

The fourth book of the Bible is so named because the first several chapters are about the census of the Jewish people.

Did you know...

That Jesus drove seven demons from Mary Magdalene (Mark 16:9).

The second name of Mary, who had been a Harlot, derives from her hometown of Magdala. She was the first person to whom Jesus appeared on the morning of his Resurrection (John 20:11-18).

And of course you know...

That the Rosary takes its name from the Latin *rosarium,* or rose garden.

Which parables are repeated in three Gospels?

The 28 different parables are told in Matthew, Mark and Luke.

There is a great deal of overlap between the parables in the Gospels, but only three parables are recounted in Matthew, Mark and Luke:

The Mustard Seed – *Matthew 13:31-32, Mark 4:31-32 and Luke 13:18-19*

The Sower – *Matthew 13:3-8, Mark 4:3-8 and Luke 8:5-8*

The Wicked Husbandman – *Matthew 21:33-34, Mark 12:1-11 and Luke 20:9-18*

How did chance keep Barsabas from becoming an Apostle?

When Peter had to select a replacement for Judas among the Apostles, he appears to have searched among the 72 disciples (Luke 10:1).

Among these, the most worthy were Matthias and Barsabas. In fact, they were so equally worthy that the only way a replacement could be chosen was by lots.

Matthias won (Acts 1:21-26).

What was Peter's Aramaic name?

It's a well-known fact that, before Jesus gave him the name Peter, the man who would become the first Pope was called Simon Bar-Jona, (Simon, son of Jona).

However, Peter is actually the Greek version of the name Jesus really gave him: His Aramaic name was Cephas, which means "a stone" (John 1:42).

Peter died in or around 67 A.D. and was succeeded by St. Linus (67-76), St. Anacletus (76-88), St. Clement (88-97), and St. Evaristus (97-105).

Through John Paul II, there have been 264 Popes in all.

What does the name Pontius Pilate mean?

Pilate was the procurator best known for being officially responsible for the condemnation of Jesus on the charge of sedition.

The name Pilate comes from the Latin *pilatus* meaning pikeman – that is, someone who carries a *pilum,* meaning a javelin.

Pilate's wife was Claudia Procula, the granddaughter of the Emperor Augustus.

What is the mysterious "Q" document?

Scholars and theologists speculate that there may have been an unknown document, or quelle (hence, "Q"), which served as a reference source for the authors of the first and the third Gospels. Such a document, it is theorized, would account for the many similarities to be found in both Matthew and Luke.

The "Q" document is presumed to have dated from the time of Jesus.

What was the angel Michael's second best-known act?

His best-known deeds revolve around his conflict with Satan (Jude 1:9, Revelation 12:7-9).

However, it was also Michael who was sent by God to tell Daniel that the Lord would protect him from the Persians (Daniel 13).

What was the greatest love in the Old Testament?

That would have to have been Jacob's love for Rachel.

According to Genesis 29, Jacob fell in love with Rachel, daughter of Laban, and agreed to work for her father for seven years in order to win her hand.

But at the end of those seven years, Laban tricked Jacob into marrying Rachel's older sister Leah.

In order to win Rachel, Jacob agreed to another seven years of servitude – though the second seven years "seemed unto him but a few days, for the love he had to her" (Genesis 29:20).

Rachel bore Jacob two sons: Joseph and Benjamin. She died giving birth to the latter (Genesis 35:18).

What are the 14 stations of the cross?

A devotion or meditation on the Passion of Christ, the stations – wooden crosses usually attached to the walls of a church symbolize:

1. His condemnation to death.

2. Bearing the cross.

3. Jesus falls.

4. Jesus meets his mother.

5. Jesus is aided by Simon.

6. Veronica wipes Jesus' face.

7. Jesus falls again.

8. Jesus comforts the women of Jerusalem.

9. Jesus falls for a third time.

10. Jesus is stripped.

11. Jesus is placed on the cross.

12. Jesus dies.

13. Jesus is taken down from the cross.

14. Jesus is placed in his tomb.

Why is the Latin Bible called Vulgate?

The Latin translation of the Bible was commissioned by Pope St. Damasus I in 382 and executed by St. Jerome. The term comes from the Latin *vulgata* and it means the popular edition. Vulgata is derived from the Latin *vulgus* which means "common people." In other words, the Latin Bible was for everyone.

The word vulgar also derives from *vulgus* – though, taken on a somewhat different meaning, i.e., that which is common is also crude.

Here a Herod, there a Herod...

The New Testament is full of Herods.

The most famous is arguably Herod Antipas, who had John the Baptist imprisoned and also questioned the captive Jesus. After ruling from to 39 A.D., Herod was banished by the Emperor Caligula.

Herod Antipas' father was Herod the Great, King of the Jews from 37 B.C. to 4 B.C. He was succeeded by his oldest surviving son Herod Archelaus, an incompetent man who ruled for 10 years before Rome had him banished to Gaul.

Herod Philip was the third, youngest and most intelligent son of Herod the Great. During the reigns of his two brothers, he was in charge of the provinces of Iturea, Gaulanitis and Trachonitis. He died in 34 A.D.

Herod Agrippa I, king of the same regions as Herod Philip, was the son of Aristobulus, the brother of Herodias (Philip's wife). He was mur-

dered at the age of 34 while trying to negotiate a treaty with the cities of Tyre and Sidon.

Herod Agrippa II, the son of the first Agrippa, ruled his father's regions as well as Chalcis and Galilee. He died in 92 A.D.

Where was Corinth?

The Biblical book Corinthians is addressed to the devout and faithless of Corinth.

Corinth was the capital of the Roman province of Achaia in the southern part of Greece. It was a powerful and very rich city that controlled the ports of Lechaeum and Cenchreae on the west and east, respectively.

And who were the Galatians?

Paul's writings to the Galatians are a magnificent, inspiring plea for freedom, and also a diatribe against religious practices that are extraneous to the teachings of Jesus.

Galatia was a kingdom on the southern coast of the Black Sea. The Romans later expanded it, absorbing towns on the Mediterranean Sea.

What was Caiaphas' first name?

The name Caiaphas was a surname: Joseph was his first name.

Caiaphas was the Jewish high priest who was an adversary of Jesus.

What does the name "Galilee" mean?

It comes from the Hebrew word *galil,* which

means circuit. The name is taken to mean that Galilee was complete, well-defined, and more or less self-supporting.

What does the name "Israelite" mean?

In Hebrew, it means "Who prevails with God."

Are there contemporary secular references to Jesus?

There are. Most notable are a letter written by Pliny, Governor of Bithynia, and the writings of the historian Tacitus.

Both of these confirm that Jesus was a rabbi, many of whose followers believed that he was the Son of God.

Parting wisdom from the Bible

❦ "Ye ought to be quiet and do nothing rashly." – *Acts 19:36*

❦ "Before honor is humility." – *Proverbs 15:33*

❦ "A merry heart maketh a cheerful countenance." – *Proverbs 15:13*

❦ "Be not overcome of evil, but overcome evil with good." – *Romans 12:21*